Desert
Well

and Other Poems

by

Michael C. Owens

Honolulu, Hawaii

Original chapbook published December 2006

Michael C. Owens
6488 Hawaii Kai Dr., Honolulu, Hawaii 96825
mcowens@mcowens.com :: www.mcowens.com

"The Dance" was previously published online at www.poetry.com, March 2003.

ISBN 978-0-9838021-0-5

Acknowledgment: Poetry, to be done well, needs more than inspiration, insight, or facility with language. Over the last four years my writing coach and mentor, Phyllis Hoge Thompson, has patiently encouraged me to leave the shallows of verse and venture into the deeper waters of various poetic forms and a more careful attention to technical detail, and has been kind enough to rescue me on those occasions when I get in over my head. She has been of incalculable help, and I am deeply appreciative of her willingness to tolerate my flailing about in her pool of experience and expertise - Phyllis, currently a resident of Albuquerque, New Mexico, is a former Professor of English at the University of Hawaii, has published seven books of poetry, one prose memoir, and received the Hawaii Award for Literature in 1995.

As for myself and my own writing accomplishments, this first offering contains a variety of poems in a variety of styles with no particular theme and in no particular order which I sincerely hope will cause me incalculable embarrassment and pale in comparison with future offerings.

Contents

Desert Well

My thirsting led me here,
To this dry well of your sanctuary,
Aging, deep and cold, where
Capricious winds of sermons turn
The sands of stirring faith,
And pile them into shifting dunes
That wander, form, and slump
Below high heaven's searing gaze.

Where are you, now? I wrestle
Alone by an empty river, and strike
The dry rocks with my rod.
A thirsty man could perish here,
Ignored, until a mourner
Stands to light an altar candle
And speak a benediction,
To scatter his falling dust to the wind.

Or, until a woman comes
Down from her desert place,
Seeking at the well to fill,
Again, her emptied cup,

To find a water-burdened stranger,

A thirsting, dying man,

Who asks her for a drink.

And she responds, puts down her jar

Into his depths and draws

Her measure, to satisfy his thirst.

Then rising, scatters words like dust,

While he, atoned, reflects

The fruitful soil around his well.

Appeased, a man could live

Here in this fertile sanctuary.

Yet thirsting, I chase the wind.

The Dance

Eyes closed, I see
You dance in graceful sweep.
A supple frame,
Your lithe form bends and leaps -
A pirouette,
And now glissade. At last
You draw me in
And thrust me to the fore.
I grope in wonder
For the beat - harmonic
Ebb and flow.
The need vibrating now
With every surge,
With every stroke, your rhythm
I embrace.
I see, eyes closed, you dance.

Dream

We dream, where land embraces restive sea,
The emerald flash of day, a crimson flame
On upland slopes, and first star wishes stir
Spring tides that swirl around this island rim.

We sail, my hand in full command, and loose
The clinging heat of day; then trace at length
Your sheltered coves and clefts and stretching length,
A lingering course, down curving neck, to loose

Each trembling swell, then straight to harbor's rim.
Past skirting reefs and rising shoals we stir,
And stars that paced our ebb and flow soon flame
Beneath our dreams - where land embraces sea.

The Poet Galway Kinnell

You say that he defies description,
Cannot be caged with words.
A wash of applause dries before his rise,
And he stands,
Gripped behind the podium,
Black thoughts on white sheets,
Water braced and amplified,
Disorganized around a theme,
And the audience ripples into depths
Of half-attentive consciousness
And often practiced intellectual stares,
As the poet bleeds from open wounds
And feeds on the guts of bears.

Temple Valley

I've paused beside these lawns before
Where twilight blurs the distant shore,
But now I stop, and bending, brush
A fresh stone laid in the valley floor.

A name, two dates. The valley, lush
From sea born rains that end their rush
Along this curtained mountain side,
Draws close, encircling evening's hush.

So little marks life's swirling ride:
A day of birth, the day she died.
What joys between? Whose love surrounds?
Whose dreams embrace her voice inside?

Struck once, a distant bell resounds,
A longing tone that knows no bounds.
Last light. I turn to leave these grounds,
For others wait my scheduled rounds.

Seeking, Growing

Mother would put a pot to boil for eggs,
And I would watch, eager to see the first
Small bubbles form and quiver at the bottom.
Expectant, excited, straining, seeking, growing.

And soon enough a shivering release,
Replaced within a moment by another,
And again, until the whole pot roiled
With churning steam and "careful, honey" bubbles.

And then the eggs and momentary calm,
But quickly then, the heated pace resumed
Until the steam and froth obscured my view.
When done, the pot was quenched - eggs and all.

Mistral Winds

The flood of night has peaked, its ebbing flow
Sets eddies where your murmured dreams are moored.
I stir, and reach to brush your placid arm,
Not to wake, but reaffirm command -
In silence, so you can't object, or turn
Away in scorn, or shame, or discontent,
Or toward some distant, lightening horizon.

The room is still, outside the trades have calmed.
I taste your breath, the warmth of distant surf.
Why did I not understand? We joined,
Wed, and you were launched anew, grew strong,
And changed. Your course, at first, lay close to mine,
But then diverged in ways I did not see
In time, could not prevent - indeed, would not.

I'm cold. I pull the sheets and quilt around
And feel my body slowly warm. You stir,
But then are still. Reality is now -
The harbor sure, you dared the mistral winds
Alone and sailed beyond the sight of shore.
I reach, but then pull back - the helm is yours.
I wait for dawn, and dream your passage home.

Autumn's Path

And now, my autumn path. Through skirring leaves,
And tangled roots, and faint recall of spring,
What breath is left to speak? Passion's rise
And summer's flood now ebb. I bank my dreams
Against the coming deep and fitful draft.

Above, a pale, receding sky, its crystal
Cirrus heralds hint of winter's keening -
And slipping down the shaded way I feel
My whispered name brush past. A wafting breeze
Mutters resignation, and release.

But through these bracing days I reach to warm
My thoughts beside the embers of your fire.
A sullen winter shroud will be your fate,
As mine. But we have planted vision's seed,
And soon enough, the soil will dream anew.

The Mime

Contorted mime, defined by painted face
And mind, entrapped within a shrinking box.
Supple arms and practiced hands press flat,
To push away imagined closing walls.

With mimes there are no words. I cannot count
The words we spoke around our days, or wrote
When talk was done, and distance intervened.
So many words to form this silent box

Confining face and mind. The practiced mime
Stands straight when done - his box dismissed as air.
He tips his hat, though he has none, and leaves
To awkward arms and wordless hands, his work.

Faded Lilacs

My winter steps encircle silent oak
And brittle birch, and springtime lilac dreams.
In vexing light I lay a dappled cloak
Of leaves across a fading past that seems

To press upon my path. This tattered day
Shades to a close; a fretful breeze soon hints
That sullen winter gusts and sheets of gray
Will shroud the night, as purple twilight glints

Off stained glass windows, shut against the pall.
Your candle burns inside, where cup and plate
Are set, and shadows flicker down the hall,
To pause by polished brass and oak. I wait

The end of circling words, arranged and pressed,
To lay these faded lilacs at your breast.

Bright Day

Come bright day and I will wake, a poet
Robed and prostrate, rapt before your altar;
Blessed by doves that rise as wisps of morning,
Stirring through soft chimes and turning breezes.

Come bright day and I will bloom, a sun struck
Blossom bursting from the bud, my fragrance
Pulsing warm and lush, as earth and heaven's
Trysting place, among my velvet petals.

Come bright day and I will dance, embracing
Dreams, and radiance, and wind; no longer
Bound to solemn strains, my spirit, vaulting
Past the pale, shall whirl to rainbow medleys.

Deuteronomy 34: 1-8

Then Moses climbed Mount Nebo from
        the plains of Moab to the top
Of Pisgah, near to Jericho.
        And there the Lord showed him the whole,
From Gilead to Dan, and all
        of Naphtali, Ephraim,
And Manasseh, past Judah to
        the western sea, the Negev desert,
Jericho, the city known
        as Palms, as far as distant Zoar.

And then the Lord spoke straight to him:
        "This land I promised to the heirs
Of Abraham and Isaac, and to
        the sons of Jacob. I made an oath,
Which now I keep - I brought you here
        to see the dream at last fulfilled,
But you may only touch it with
        your eyes, as here your wandering ends."
Then Moses died in Moab, was buried
        in an unmarked grave, and mourned.

A found poem.

A Song for Phyllis

It's when I reach for you and find you've past,
Or speak and hear the echoes of my sigh
Down distant memories and halls, I ask,
And wait, in empty rooms, for your reply.

As if, by dreams and fancy, life again
Will charge and breech my walls, will crash and rage,
A river at its flood - to dance with sin
And laugh, immune to thoughts of death and age.

But from the shadows of this day, I feel
A shiver down my neck, as if a friend,
A lover, strong, unwavering, and real,
Arrives, as soft as falling leaves, to tend

And soothe my pain, then speaks of Delft blue skies,
And morning sunlight piercing clouded eyes.

Makapu'u

I struggle up
To where forever ends,
Abrupt and sheer above a circling sea,

And feel the rock
Trembling as I kneel,
Old and battered on a breathless ledge -

A fading beat
Beneath my fingertips -
A quiver rising, ebbing, silently.

I spread my arms
To compass sea and sky,
As if to leap and soar beyond all reach,

To skim the waves,
And wheel on lifting winds,
To dive, to breach, to ring the sun and moon,

Or else to pray,
And offer sacrifice,
To ask a blessing to stay a dying dream.

No wings but wonder,

Since memory began,

I turn to trace a scarred and weathered cliff

To where I stood,

Young, in sand and laughter.

The surge and pull of tide was gentle then -

Seductive, warm

As summer's shivering touch.

I climbed the mountain, conquered, and laid claim,

And stood resolved

Against a turning sea -

The grinding flood and drain of endless change.

The land I held,

The sea slipped by my grasp -

Elusive, enduring, overcoming all.

And now the rock

Stands shaking, worn - with sand

Its tears, the falling measure of its passing.

The Edge of Shadow

i

I pale as morning comes again, serene

And cold from night, and crackling winter skies.

A fragile light absorbs the stars, and grows

To soothe old fears, and shape familiar pasts

From lingering air still thick with fading dreams.

The dawn slips into view, and down far heights

I watch the shadow line of day advance -

A now that never was, and cannot be.

I feel what was; a thousand silken strands

Entangling light in webs both soft and strong.

I am the captor and the caught, suspended

On a fragile thread between the dark

And day that holds, cocooned, the gathered dead

Of other dawns, now hollow husks, yet living

Still in me. I cannot be what was.

I run the edge of shadow, chasing life.

ii

I rise as evening comes again, intense

From fires of day that quickly fade to ash.

Along the broad horizon hues cascade,

Descending into black, obscuring shapes
Of things I thought I knew, and raising fears.
What dreams are left have gathered close around.
The day retreats behind a line of shadows -
A now that cannot be, and never was.

I see what comes, along the glinting thread,
And yet I turn to catch at time, to flee
The chilling cold, escape the scorching heat.
But I am caught, and struggle in a web
That holds the gathered life of other dusks.
I hang suspended, still, and although now
I am not what will be, I will become.
I run the edge of shadow, chasing life.

George, The Neighbor's Cat

George, the neighbor's cat, is getting older.
Still, he stalks the birds that mock his efforts.
Sometimes futile efforts. He gets lucky.
Not with birds too often - lizards mostly,
Sunning on the nearby redwood fencing.

Stretching, preening, watching mynahs fencing
Raucously, George checks - the shadows, mostly.
Calculating angles, feeling lucky,
Crouching, tensing, twitching tail. His efforts
Fail. The birds leave laughing. George grows older.

Columbia 2003

Ashes.
Burning passions,
And tears to blind the sun.
I clap to wake the gods, and rail
Against the ash streaked sky, smoke on blue.
Then joss sticks, prayer paper, red
And gold for luck and wealth.
Burnt offerings.
Ashes.

01 February 2003, Chinese New Year, the start of the Year of the Ram (or Sheep); new moon. At 0900 hrs EST the space shuttle Columbia broke apart on descent at 207,135 feet over Texas after completing her 28th mission, killing all seven astronauts aboard.

For the dragon, Katarina Imamura

The Dragon and the Eagle

A backpack, pink shirt, bright eyes and attitude.
Direct and pure, "An eagle is on your shirt."
     "Yes, you're right, there is." I thought, and said
     "I see a dragon on yours. Do you know dragons?"
The nod was quick and firm. "There's black and red,"
She paused for thought, "and pink and green ones too."
A five year old with all the facts, so sure.
"And blue."
No questions, doubts, or hesitations.
"And fire." Wonder. "Fire comes out of their mouth."
     "And do your dragons fly? Not all dragons …."
"Of course they do." Impatient. "Dragons have wings.
They fly around." There seemed no room to argue.
"Lift me up." Assertive. Assumptive. Trusting.
She raised her arms as if to fly, majestic
Little dragon, rising
Below an aging eagle,
And I, slowly descending, obliged.

24

Baghdad

The moon. It wasn't there when I first looked.
Obscured perhaps, by shrouds of dust and smoke.
But crying in the streets at three a.m.
I shudder in the cold and pray its rise.

Nothing stirs. No echoes ripple outward.
Sand and litter, scraps of harried hours,
Shifting, drifting into empty alleys,
Settle on stone sills and shuttered windows.

This half-moon night is harsh and vexing, cold
As vengeance, stark as logic's black and white.
No acts of absolution, shades of gray,
Bars judgment's wrath, and no one cries alarm.

Gift of God? What pride consumes this city?
Fired with passion, Babel struck for heaven,
Fell in ruin, then as now. Eternal
Passions flare, to turn all hope to ashes.

What brought me here, reflecting in the cold
Reflected light of half a moon above,
As drifting ashes settle at my feet?
The waning moon, and from my depths, a scream.

Baghdad derives from the Sanskrit Bhaga-dada, meaning Gift of God.
Babel (Babil) is just south of Baghdad.

Son Light

I see in you
    a mirror,
A visual echo

Of who I was,
    just now -
Polished brass.

"I once thought that,"
    reflective.
Mercurial, time

Slips down silvered
    edges.
Fleeting light

Flickers off
    the past.
Transient flecks

Of memory,
    fleeing
Thoughts incarnate.

Passion

Is this an Easter morning? Drab and cold,
A drizzling rain holds back the coming dawn.
Obscuring clouds deny the sun and moon
Their rise and set, make vague what should be bold.

The swash of tires crossing nearby streets
Disturbs my thought, as mounting gray winds grieve
Through power lines and trees, down road scarred hills,
Around this clutch of houses, amber lit

And sealed. Like sterile eggs in sectioned crates,
Hard boiled and dyed, then hid for children's sake.
Such barren pleasure; somber passion. Yet
The world will soon leave April, greener for it.

The Male of the Species

I read about sestinas so I thought that I might try one,
But realized that if I did I might be pushed to two.
So bucking up I took a breath and counted up to three,
And soon the clicking of the keys absorbed my time 'til four.
My wife was none too happy as we had a date at five,
And though I had to rush and change, we dined as planned at six.

I saw as pure coincidence our party totaled six,
"We're six at six!" I told the group, and smiled at every one.
"But it's so early," said my wife, "we had to leave by five,
But that's okay, I've got some news - I'm eating now for two."
I used to play some football and got hit on first and four,
A blindside shot that cracked a rib, was carried off by three.

Inhaling wine feels much the same. I choked "we'll soon be three!?"
"That's right," my dearest darling said, "I'm due November six."
I sat in silence for a while, then told the other four,
"Please, no offense, we have to go, I need to think on this one."
They smiled and waved as we went out, we were the final two
Of our small group to have a child - the others had borne five.

As we drove home I kept my speed well under fifty-five.
It wouldn't do to risk a crash, in view of number three.

I thought, "if due November six, less nine, conceived at two,
So February had to be ... hmmm ... I was gone for six ..."
"My dear," I said with some concern, "explain to me this one:
My business trip went Feb the first and ended March one four ..."

"Oh, that," she said, "it's forty weeks, and plus or minus four,
And even then it's not precise. I've checked, let's see, with five
MDs to know I'm right ," she paused. "Now you explain this one:
Your business trip went well you said, but ending at week three
Your secretary left for home. Her schedule called for six.
We had a fairly lengthy chat when she returned, us two."

The car was warm, I tried to think, what had they said, those two?
"You needn't worry, dear," she said, "the switch took only four
Of those five docs to do, we were released before day six,
There wasn't any pain." Confused? My speed topped sixty-five.
"The child in me is yours," she sighed. "Although it took me three
Whole days of thought to make that choice. It took her only one."

"Her husband's six foot six," she mused, "and you are five foot two,
So we agreed to switch each one, to satisfy all four."
I frowned. I'm really five foot five. Well, maybe five foot three.

The Tao of Now

You circle round the now of time; a life
Forever passing - parting as a knife
Might cleave the whole in two - what was, what comes.
Like pi, now is and yet is not, precise:
A point without a place, a strange device,
Irrational, where future ends, becomes

What was, where past begins, and so becomes
What never was. Past memory is life.
Now is indeed a finely honed device,
Its edge as keen as found on any knife.
Although with time we seek to be precise,
And ever thinly slice the hour that comes,

We soon are cutting air. For that which comes,
Arrives, and instantly is past - becomes
Excuse or honor, fading quickly, precise
In hindsight only - afterimage life,
As fleeting as the glint off flensing knife
That seeks to flay the skin from time's device.

As truth, now is a diplomat's device:

"We'll wait and see," and when it finally comes,

"What's done is done," says he who holds the knife.

As fickle, blameless fate, now soon becomes

The place where hope joins with defeat. As life,

Now marks the start of future's past, precise

As pi the ever finer slice, precise

As truth or fate, precise as love's device,

Or hate. Precise as we would make it. Life

Is now. We choose to wait for that which comes,

Or choose to chase our hope, that which becomes.

Our choices form the cutting edge, the knife

That sculpts, creates and forms, our past. The knife

Of now, the blade of time, its fall precise

As dawn's advance, which circling round becomes

Advancing dusk. This marvelous device

Called now - the shadow of what future comes,

Reflection of what's past - exists as life.

As fast as hope becomes, it's past. Time's knife

Is now, that slices life in two. Precise

And strange device, to mark what was, what comes.

The Rain

The rain will be here soon. I feel its weight,
Its brooding presence. Life seeks shelter. Hides.
A distant rumble speaks of unsure fate.

As vision fails, the world beyond my gate
Dissolves like footprints swept by fading tides.
The rain will be here soon. I feel its weight,

Inhale its breath, as if possessed by hate
Or love. Dark passions swirl, embrace both sides.
A distant rumble speaks of unsure fate,

The certainty of change. And as I wait
Among new ruined choirs, hope abides.
The rain will be here soon. I feel its weight,

A heavy, breathless charge. No more debate
As one drop streaks the glass. All thought subsides.
A distant rumble speaks of unsure fate.

No rant nor rage averts this storm. Too late
To plant or reap. On hope the future rides.
The rain will be here soon. I feel its weight.
A distant rumble speaks of unsure fate.

As If To Fly

Such wonders as a wing swept granite peak,
A snow framed mountain lake, or sun streaked leaf,
Arouses deep inside my searching core
So vast a calm, I struggle just to speak.
And then I rise and dance through a too small house,
Arms stretched, as if to fly.

As surging waves carve fluted cliffs and caves,
And thunder over fringing coral reef,
My breaching soul sings out to distant shore,
My thrumming spirit sounds a cry, and raves.
And then I rise and dance through a too small house,
Arms stretched, as if to fly.

As space and stars and distant planets spin,
Erupt and flare, and loose the bonds of dream,
I search this turning galaxy for more,
For wondrous shapes and songs concealed within.
And then I rise and dance through a too small house,
Arms stretched, as if to fly.

Where eagles, whales, and celestial dragons play,
I soar and dive and ride a radiant stream
Of sun flecked thought through wonder's silent door
Across the sky to greet the light of day.
And then I rise and dance through a too small house,
Arms stretched, as if to fly.

Choosing

i

"I need to know, did I choose right?" she asked.

And I replied, "You chose, and that was right."

"But what I choose must matter ..."

"Of course. To you."

"But others ..."

"Again, of course. But they choose, too."

ii

And swiftly, down a crowded road, I came

to where it split,

And in a rush considered left or right,

which way to go.

And choosing turned along that way, went on,

committed now.

And soon enough, too soon perhaps, again

I saw once more.

And choosing, I again went on, again

I chose, again.

And coming to a lonely stretch I slowed

enough to ask

And argue with myself, "Did I choose right?

Is this the way?"

And fancied what I missed, what could have been,

how life would change,

And never thought that I would ask this same

on other roads

And other places, now and later. Would

again, would here

And there, no matter where I ended up

or found myself.

iii

I chose, like you, and that is all that matters.

Kuykendall Hall, University of Hawaii

Ananda asked Kassapa, "Buddha gave you the golden robe of
successorship. What else did he give you?"
Kassapa said, "Ananda."
Ananda answered, "Yes, brother."
Said Kassapa, "Now you can take down my preaching sign and put up
your own."

i

Outside, the reigning heat of summer's day.
In here, the cool release of Kuykendall.

ii

I choose to be one with the building. It's Saturday - early.
I'm waiting for the key, a campus guard
To come unlock my third floor classroom door.

I stand alone in the hall, eyes closed - breathing in,
Breathing out. My posture shifts as muscles relax
And body straightens, adjusts. Head erect,
Releasing thought, I drift back on my heels.

Awareness. A distant hum, and air that sighs
Behind a ceiling vent. Suspended motes
Of idle thought wander through the moment -
Golden flecks of insight, briefly caught
In logic's light - fleeting wisps of reason.

iii

I calm myself from the center out, and the hall
Is suddenly filled with clattering talk and laughter

As doors swing open and students rush room to room.
I open my eyes - the hall is empty and still,

Except the hum and vibration of air conditioning.
I close my eyes again, regain repose.
Breathing in. Breathing out. Empty as the hall.

iv
I hear the guard's approach and clash of keys.
Wordless, he opens the door, then leaves. I enter,

Arrange the chairs, and chalk my name on the board.

If You Were A Cat

If
you
were a cat
I'd bring you a rat,
dead, and dangling
from my lips.
A gray one - fat.
I'd drop it at your feet,
then sit and lick my paws,
preening fur and whiskers,
thinking you might like that.
However, you are not a cat,
and so I bring you flowers,
then sit, as I stroke my chin,
while wondering at my luck.
It isn't all that hard to stalk
and pluck a pretty flower.
I think it's very sweet
that you don't want
a big, dead,

g
r
a
y
r
a
t
.

Season's End

Sand, wind, and chimes - late summer porch.
I watch the sun-catcher's languid turn and glint,
Framed by window sash and curtain lace.

Waves and thoughts along the long shoreline
Rise up, rush in, then vanish in the sand,
Stranding flotsam, foam, and scurrying crabs.

God's breath is drawn, the ocean's calm. Yet storms
Are brewing south and east - familiar ache
In brittle, dried out bones, carelessly tossed

In my immortal youth - readable now.
Too late to shutter the house. Let it go.
I will to the wind my dust - the dross of all

My hoarded memories, the husks of dreams,
Abandoned passions, lost in cluttered cupboards,
Chests, and barren windrows, distracting thought.

Shards of sunlight, gold and red, glance
From lace topped waves and slowly turning glass,
Bound by window, porch, and fading wind.

Primitive

Youth's fury writhes -
Insatiable fire -
Its spirit caught
In obsidian.
Primitive,
Like ritual dance,
A swirling frieze.

Passion flares,
Erupts, consumes -
Trysts with death.
Desire exults,
Despair laments,
Embraces pain,
And craves release.

The dark veined stone
Is struck and split -
Its glistening blade,
Exposed, descends.
Released, the fires
Consume and spread,
Devour all.

City People

City People I

Scattered slips of insight gild stone walls,
Quiver over concrete, steel, and glass -
Shattered mirrors clutched in broken frames,
Shiver through these streets, reflect, then pass.

City People II

Crystal glints and spectral twists of thought,
Splintered echoes, images entrance,
Glacial sunlight, cold as fractured ice,
Captured in a moment's twitch and dance.

Perchance To Dream

Say morning comes again, and I awake
To fading strains of half remembered song,
And you are still beside me, strangely calm,
As if some darkling fantasy had sought
To free your restive spirit, in silence caught
Your outstretched arms, then whispered you away.

I shiver in this empty cave of morning,
Where dreams are laid and hope has not yet risen,
A pale, suspended place, too soon forsaken,
And yet not soon enough - for here is silence,
A nothingness that drains my hollow presence,
A hush that chases fleeting wisps of meaning.

I reach for you, for life that fades unseen -
Uncertain - wrestling emptiness and doubts.
An ebbing warmth and hopeless afterthoughts
Are all that linger in this shadowed cold -
And shaken, I awake, confused and old,
To find you still beside me, caught in dream.

Elegy For The Present

This lagoon at noon
      rippled turquoise, pelagic blue,
           and sand -
soft coral sand, not granite grit or stone.
Summer sounds rose warm
      as a lover's voice;
        soft and fragrant, sweet
as mangos in the morning,
           afterwards.

At night we caught
      at brief phosphorescent
         sparks of life -
held starlight in our hands
         that faded as we watched
before a rising moon.
We wished upon an evening star
      and vowed
         to live the day and not look back.

Now our words have grayed and winter's come;
the beach holds nothing of our past but dreams.